My Little Story of Christmas

Karen Williamson
Illustrated by Amanda Enright

In the village of Nazareth there lived a young woman named Mary.

One day, the angel Gabriel appeared to her.
"You are going to have a very special baby," he said.
"God wants you to call him Jesus."

Mary loved Joseph, the village carpenter.
Now they decided to get married.

Mary went to see her cousin Elizabeth.
"I'm going to have a baby boy," said Mary.
Elizabeth was expecting a baby too.
They were both very happy.

Joseph and Mary had to travel to the town of Bethlehem.
It was a long, hard journey.
Mary was very tired when at last they arrived.

Then a kindly innkeeper said,
"I have a little stable. You can stay there if you like."

So Jesus was born in a borrowed stable in Bethlehem.
The donkeys and cows watched quietly.
Mary laid baby Jesus gently to sleep in the animals' manger.

Some shepherds were minding their sheep in fields nearby.
Suddenly they saw a bright light – and an angel appeared.
"Tonight a baby is born in Bethlehem," he said.
"He has come to save his people."

Then lots of angels appeared.
"Praise God in heaven!" they sang.
"Peace on earth!"

The shepherds rushed off to find the newborn baby. When they reached the stable in Bethlehem, they knelt before Jesus.

In a distant land, some wise men noticed a new star in the sky. "Let's follow this star," they said. "It will lead us to a newborn baby. One day he will be a king."

The wise men journeyed many miles.
They rode by night so they could follow the star.

After many adventures, the wise men finally arrived at the town of Bethlehem. There the star stopped.

The wise men soon found little Jesus. They knelt before him.
They gave him rich presents: gold, frankincense,
and a perfume called myrrh.

When Jesus was a bit older, Mary and Joseph took him back home to Nazareth.

There Jesus grew up. He helped Joseph in his carpenter's shop. He played with his friends and helped his mother.
Jesus was getting ready for the special job God had for him.